CONCRETE
Creations

First published in Great Britain in 2018

Search Press Limited
Wellwood, North Farm Road,
Tunbridge Wells, Kent TN2 3DR

Original editions ©: 2015/2016
World rights reserved by Christophorus Verlag GmbH, Rheinfelden/Germany
Original German titles: *Wohnaccessoires aus Beton selber machen* and
Kreativ mit Beton: Kleine Projekte zum Selbermachen

English translation by Burravoe Translation Services

Photographs and styling by Uli Glasemann, Roland Krieg and Elke Reith

Design copyright © Search Press Ltd., 2018

ISBN: 978-1-78221-585-1

PUBLISHER'S NOTE
The Publishers and author can accept no responsibility for any
consequences arising from the information, advice or instructions given in
this publication.

Readers are permitted to reproduce any of the items in this book for their
personal use, or for the purposes of selling for charity, free of charge and
without the prior permission of the Publishers. Any use of the items for
commercial purposes is not permitted without the prior permission of
the Publishers.

SUPPLIERS
If you have difficulty in obtaining any of the materials and equipment
mentioned in this book, then please visit the Search Press website for
details of suppliers at searchpress.com

CONTRIBUTORS: Marion Dawidowski (pages 18-21, 30/1, 34/5, 36/7, 80/1,
84/5, 86-89, 96/7, 108/9); Annette Diepolder (pages 14/5, 42/3, 48/9,
52-55, 62/3, 66/7, 74/5, 82/3); Simea Gut (pages 16/7, 40/1, 44/5, 46/7,
56/7, 60/1, 64/5); Ingrid Moras (pages 72/3, 76-79, 90/1, 94/5, 98-101,
104/5, 106/7, 110-113, 114/5, 116/7, 118/9); Elke Reith (pages 28/9,
32/3, 38/9) and Sybille Rogaczewski-Nogai (pages 26/7, 50/1, 58/9, 68/9).

Printed in China by 1010 Printing International Ltd

CONCRETE
Creations

45 EASY-TO-MAKE GIFTS & ACCESSORIES

**MARION DAWIDOWSKI,
INGRID MORAS
& OTHERS**

SEARCH PRESS

Contents

Why concrete?

In the past, concrete was considered to be cold and coarse; nobody could imagine using it for anything beyond construction work, let alone to create pieces for the home.

But now this exciting material has shed its old image as its numerous underrated qualities have been brought to the fore: concrete is decorative, flexible, economical and tough. In addition, it is very eco-friendly because it contains only natural components and can be recycled with few problems.

So it is no surprise that concrete is becoming an increasingly popular material for making items for the house and garden. With few resources and no extensive craft skills or prior knowledge, it is possible to create impressive decorative objects made of concrete to display proudly in your home. The items you can make can be elegant and timeless, pure and simple or modern and playful; there are no limits to your creativity. This book will show you how to make them, along with beautiful photographs to inspire you to start your own concrete journey.

Working with concrete

The right material makes all the difference

Nowadays, it is possible to buy a range of different types of concrete mix if you want to use concrete in a creative way. In order to achieve a great result quickly, premixed concrete is the best thing to use because you do not need to spend time mixing the individual ingredients together: simply add water to the quick mix, stir it and off you go. Ready-mixed concrete is available from most DIY stores, craft shops and on the Internet.

Concrete comes in a variety of grain sizes, which allows you to achieve different textures: if you want an especially fine finish you should choose fine-grained concrete screed, or pass the ready-mixed concrete through a fine sieve to remove any unwanted stones. If you want a rougher texture for the item you are making, leave the small stones in the mix. Quick-set concrete is not advisable for the projects in this book, especially if you are new to concrete, because it sets too quickly.

Special craft concrete, such as Beton für Kreative by Viva Decor and Concrete Craft by Creativ, is used for some of the projects in this book – for jewellery in particular – and is available online and in some specialist craft stores. It is very fine-grained, quick-drying, produces less dust, and is suitable especially for plastic, papier-mâché, wood and silicone moulds.

Concrete-effect paste is also used for a small selection of the projects, and creates an effective concrete appearance for fragile items.

Suitable moulds

Many different materials are suitable to use as moulds for concrete. Receptacles made of plastic or strong cardboard are best for making concrete models, but moulds made of wood, silicone, rubber or metal can also be used. Baking trays, storage containers, bowls, disposable crockery, plastic bottles, yoghurt pots, juice or milk cartons, and many other types of packaging can be used as moulds. Nowadays, special moulds for concrete are also available commercially.

The important thing is that the mould is strong and that you brush it carefully with a separating agent such as cooking oil before adding the mixture. This makes it easier to remove the concrete object later. Other materials are also effective at releasing the concrete item, such as petroleum jelly, cling film (plastic wrap) and foil.

If you have used cardboard for your moulds, it can simply be torn off once the concrete is dry. Some plastic moulds which are tapered towards the opening, such as bottles, usually need to be cut off to remove the newly made concrete item.

Basic equipment needed for your concrete designs

Moulds made of modelling foam

Modelling foam (such as Styrofoam™) is particularly suitable for producing highly individual concrete moulds. Modelling foam is a thermoplastic material which is used frequently in the building trade and by modellers. Since it is a solid foam material, it is very easy to cut out moulds from it using a scroll saw, a jigsaw with a very fine blade or a regular craft knife.

When working with modelling foam, it is important that the material is not stuck together with solvent-based adhesive – especially when producing moulds consisting of several sections – as this type of adhesive eats unwanted holes into the material. Moulds made from modelling foam can be finished by rubbing them down with fine-grained sandpaper, which will smooth out any uneven areas.

Concrete items that have been made using modelling foam are best removed from the moulds by cutting the foam with a craft knife and then breaking it off.

9

Mixing concrete – it's really simple

Once you have the right mould and have brushed it with cooking oil, the next step is mixing the concrete. It is best to do this outside, or on a well-covered table, as some of it may spill.

For mixing, you will a need a bucket or bowl, and a spoon or whisk to stir the mixture and water. The mixing ratio of concrete to water is given by the manufacturer on the packet. Unfortunately, it is impossible to mix up the exact amount of concrete for the project you have chosen. You can, however, use a little trick to calculate the approximate amount: fill the mould with water and mix this quantity with the correct proportion of ready-mix concrete.

The required consistency of the concrete often depends on the object you are making. For some projects, you will need thicker concrete (e.g. the door stop on page 42); for others, especially finer concrete objects, you should be careful not to make the concrete mixture too thick.

Filling the mould

When pouring the concrete into the mould, you need to make sure to spread the mixture well into all the corners. After pouring the concrete in, it is best to tap the mould on the table and shake it a little to prevent air bubbles from forming later.

After you have poured in the mixture, the bucket, spoon and all other equipment used should be thoroughly cleaned immediately; this is because once it has set, it is almost impossible to remove the concrete.

After filling the mould you will need to wait. How long an object needs to set depends on its size and thickness, and the concrete mix used. Some concrete mixes from craft shops set very quickly. It usually takes two to three days until it is completely set. The object needs to stay in its mould for at least one day in any case, so that it does not break when it is removed. To dry the object you should put it in a cool, dry place. The surface should also be level so that the concrete mixture can spread evenly; you can use a spirit level if necessary to check this.

Further tips and tricks

- For larger concrete items, we recommend that you use a drill with a mixer attachment to prepare the concrete mixture.

- If you are using a thick plastic bottle as a mould, cut through the bottle about two-thirds of the way up, so you are left with both a bottom and a top piece. Stick the bottle back together again with strong sticky tape, making sure the pieces line up as much as possible. You can then proceed to fill the bottle with concrete. This will make it easier for you to remove the object from the mould once it is dry. If this causes fine moulding seams on the surface, these can be trimmed off with the blade of a craft knife, or rubbed down with sandpaper.

- Cooking oil spray is particularly good for oiling your moulds. Although it is a little more expensive than cooking oil bought in normal bottles, it can help to ensure that even the smallest crevices are covered with oil.

- Once you have removed the object from its mould, you can rub down irregular surfaces, rough areas or seams using fine-grained sandpaper.

- In order to prevent the concrete objects from scratching the furniture or the floor, it is a good idea to stick self-adhesive felt gliders on the base of the finished object. You can buy these in various shapes and colours.

10

HEALTH AND SAFETY

- When handling large volumes of concrete inside, it is important that the room is as effectively ventilated as possible to ensure absolute respiratory protection.

- In order to protect your hands from drying out and irritation, it is important to wear strong gloves such as ones made from rubber.

- It is advisable to wear eye protection and a dust mask throughout the mixing and moulding of your concrete pieces.

- It is recommended also to wear good, impermeable, protective clothing to avoid direct contact with concrete.

- Do not use any moulds for food preparation after pouring concrete in them.

- After you have finished making your items, wash your hands thoroughly with clean water.

THE PROJECTS

Candle holders

Materials

What you need:

- **Concrete mix**
- **Rectangular plastic mould, 13 x 5.5 x 5cm (5 x 2¼ x 2in)**
- **Square plastic mould, 5.5 x 5.5cm (2¼ x 2¼in)**
- **2 plastic pipes, 2cm (¾in) in diameter, 10cm (4in) long**
- **Plastic corks, 2cm (¾in) long**
- **2 blocks of wood, one 12 x 5 x 1.8cm (4¾ x 2 x ⅝in) and the other 4.5cm (1¾in) cube**
- **White and black craft paints and paint brush**
- **Toothbrush**
- **Silicone adhesive**
- **Cooking oil and brush**
- **Drill and masonry bit**
- **Bowl**

Step 3

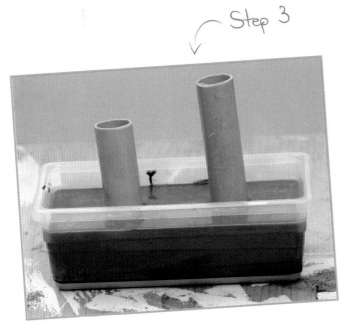

What to do:

1. Cut the corks in half, and use them to plug one end of each of the pieces of pipe.

2. Brush the moulds and the pieces of pipe with some cooking oil.

3. Add water to the concrete mix and pour the mixture into the two prepared moulds. Place the pieces of pipe, spaced evenly with the closed end downwards, into the rectangular mould to create the recesses for the candles. Leave the concrete to set for several days. Remove the concrete item from the plastic mould and extract the pipes.

4. Drill a hole 2cm (¾in) in diameter in the square block of wood to hold the candle. Prime both blocks of wood with white paint and allow to dry. Dip the toothbrush into the black paint, and run your fingers over the bristles to flick the black onto the blocks of wood. We recommend you do some sprinkle tests beforehand on a piece of paper.

5. Once they are dry, stick the concrete and wooden sections together with silicone adhesive: for the double candle holder, glue the concrete onto the wooden block; for the single candle holder, glue the wooden block onto the concrete.

Cutlery sign

What you need:

- **Concrete mix**
- **Silicone spoon mould, approx. 17 x 12cm (6¾ x 4¾in)**
- **White frame with rigid back, approx. 30 x 20 x 3cm (11¾ x 7¾ x 1¼in)**
- **Alphabet stamp set**
- **Black ink pad**
- **Hot melt glue and glue gun**
- **Cooking oil and brush**
- **Sandpaper**

What to do:

1. Brush the mould with cooking oil. Add water to the concrete mix and fill the mould with the mixture. Leave the concrete to set for several days.

2. Once dry, carefully remove the object from the mould. If the edge is uneven, rub it down with sandpaper.

3. Put the concrete object in the centre of the frame and fix it in place with the hot adhesive. Stamp out the letters 'Kitchen Stories', or the text you want, in black ink.

Tip:

If you do not have a stamp, use a computer to print out the text you want onto a piece of paper – or even cut out letters from a newspaper – and then stick them onto the frame.

Step 1

Desk Organiser

I JUST WANT TO
DRINK COFFEE
CREATE STUFF
AND SLEEP

Pen holders

What you need:

- **Concrete mix**
- **1 plastic bottle, 1.5l (2½pints)**
- **2 plastic cups, 200ml (6¾fl oz)**
- **Cooking oil and brush**
- **Scissors or craft knife**
- **General purpose adhesive**
- **Pebbles to use as a weight**

What to do:

1. Cut the plastic bottles down to a height of 10cm (4in) and brush them with cooking oil on the inside; brush the plastic cups with oil on the outside. Add water to the concrete mix.

2. For the version with horizontal grooves (the bottom section of the bottle), fill the mould with concrete until half full. Press the plastic cup into the middle so that the rim of the cup is level with the rim of the mould. Weigh it down with pebbles and then fill up the remaining space with the concrete mixture, around the cup and up to the rim. Leave the concrete to set for several days.

3. Once it is dry, cut the mould and pull it off. The edges can be rubbed down with sandpaper.

4. For the version with vertical grooves (the upper section of the bottle), apply the glue to the inside edge of the cup rim and stick it to the bottle opening. Once the glue is dry, turn your mould with the affixed plastic cup upside down and fill the mould with concrete mix. Leave to set.

← Step 1

Pen dish

What you need:

- **Concrete mix**
- **Plastic container, 11.5 x 18cm, 4cm high (4½ x 7in, 1½in high)**
- **Old rigid glasses case**
- **Duct tape**
- **Cooking oil and brush**
- **Pebbles to use as a weight**

What to do:

1. Place some pebbles in the glasses case to weigh it down. Mask the case with sticking tape to protect it from damage and to cover the opening. Brush one side of it with cooking oil, and then oil the plastic mould.

2. Add water to the concrete mix and pour into the plastic mould to a depth of about 3cm (1¼in). Press the oiled side of the spectacle case up to halfway into the wet mixture.

3. Once dry, take the spectacle case out of the concrete and remove the concrete shape from the mould.

Tip:

An empty ice cream carton makes a particularly good mould for the pen dish.

Step 2

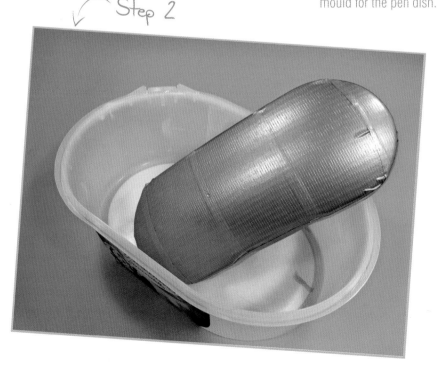

Numbered plant pot

What you need:

- **Concrete mix**
- **Small bucket, approx. 18cm (7in) in diameter**
- **Empty plastic tape roll**
- **Numbers made of foam rubber or sponge**
- **Plastic plant pot, approx. 12cm (4¾in) in diameter**
- **Cooking oil and brush**
- **Brush**
- **Glue stick**
- **Sand to use as a weight**

What to do:

1. Stick the numbers in reverse onto the inside surface of the bucket. Once dry, brush the numbers and the inside of the bucket with cooking oil.

2. Place the tape roll into the middle of the bucket. Add water to the concrete mix and pour the mixture into the mould up to the top of the tape roll. Then, stand the plastic plant pot on top of it, weigh it down with sand and fill the rest of the bucket with the concrete mix up to the rim of the plant pot. Leave the concrete to set for several days.

3. Once it has set, carefully lift the concrete plant pot out of the bucket and remove the numbers from the surface.

Tip:

Alternatively, you can make the numbers yourself. Print out the numbers in the desired font and size, transfer them to foam rubber and cut them out.

Materials

Step 2

Wall art & candle holders

What you need – Wall art:

- **Concrete mix**
- **Plastic plant pot saucer, approx. 22cm (8¾in) in diameter**
- **White, apricot and light blue craft paints**
- **Paint brush**
- **Cooking oil and brush**
- **Drill and masonry bit**
- **Masking tape**

What you need – Candle holders:

- **Concrete mix**
- **2 disposable cardboard cups**
- **2 tealights**
- **White, apricot and light blue craft paints**
- **Paint brush**
- **Cooking oil and brush**
- **Coins to use as weights**
- **Masking tape**

What to do – Wall art:

1. Brush the plant pot saucer with cooking oil and fill it with concrete to a depth of approximately 2.5cm (1in).

2. Leave the concrete to set for several days and then remove it from the plant pot saucer mould.

3. Drill a notch into the back of the wall decoration to hang it up.

4. Make a pattern on the front: using masking tape to create a negative impression of your desired design on the concrete, paint in the gaps and then peel away the tape to reveal your pattern.

What to do – Candle holders:

1. Take the candles out of their cases. Brush the outsides of the cases with plenty of cooking oil and add water to the concrete mix.

2. Pour the concrete mixture into the disposable cups to different levels. Press the tealight cases into the middle of the concrete, so that they are level with the top of the concrete. Weigh down with coins.

3. Leave the concrete to set for several days and then remove the objects from the moulds: pull out the tealight cases and tear off the disposable cups.

4. Decorate the objects with the desired pattern using masking tape and paint with the craft paints.

Tip:

The craft paints should be as thick as possible, so they do not run down the concrete.

Step 2

Wall clock

What you need:

- **Concrete mix**
- **Mini quiche dish, 15–20cm (6–7¾in) in diameter**
- **Disposable cup, approx. 7cm (2¾in) in diameter**
- **Clock mechanism**
- **Clock hands**
- **Superglue**
- **Black felt-tip pen**
- **Cooking oil and brush**
- **Drill and masonry bit**
- **Fine-grained sandpaper**

What to do:

1. Brush the inside of the quiche dish mould and the outside of the cup with cooking oil.

2. Add water to the concrete mix. Half-fill the quiche dish with concrete; press the cup into the middle, standing upright, so that it almost touches the bottom.

3. Leave the concrete to set for several days. Remove the cup from the middle first, then press the disc shape out of the quiche dish mould. Rub down the rough edges with sandpaper.

4. Drill a hole in the middle of the disc and stick the clock mechanism on the back in the recessed area; attach the hands to the front of the clock and push them onto the clock mechanism. Drill a notch into the back of the clock, about halfway through the concrete, and approximately 1.5cm (½in) in from the middle of the upper edge in order to hang it.

5. Draw in twelve lines on the clock face with the felt-tip pen. Tighten the clock mechanism and the hands.

Step 4

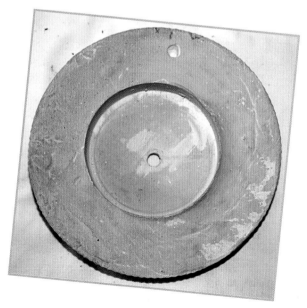

Letters

What you need:

- Concrete mix
- Cardboard letter moulds R, E, L, A and X, or as desired, approx. 15cm (6in) high
- Craft knife
- Sandpaper

Step 1

What to do:

1. Carefully remove the back covers of the individual letters using a craft knife.

2. Add water to the concrete mix and pour the mixture into the individual letters. Shake them a little to release any air bubbles and to flatten the surface. If necessary, smooth out the surface with a spatula.

3. Leave the concrete to set for several days. Then carefully tear off the cardboard on all sides and rub down any rough or uneven edges with sandpaper.

Step 2

Magnets

What you need:

- **Concrete mix**
- **Ice cube tray**
- **2 flat magnets per mould, 1mm (1/32in) thick, 6mm (1/4in) in diameter**
- **Epoxy adhesive, or similar resin and hardener**
- **Cooking oil and brush**
- **Brush**

What to do:

1. Brush the ice cube tray with cooking oil. Add water to the concrete mix; the consistency should be pulpy but not runny.

2. Gradually fill the ice cube tray mould with concrete mixture, constantly tapping it on the work surface so that any trapped air is released and the surface becomes flat. Leave the concrete to set for several days.

3. Press the concrete shapes out of the tray. The edges and surfaces can be rubbed down with sandpaper if necessary.

4. Attach two magnets on one side of each of the concrete shapes using epoxy adhesive.

Materials

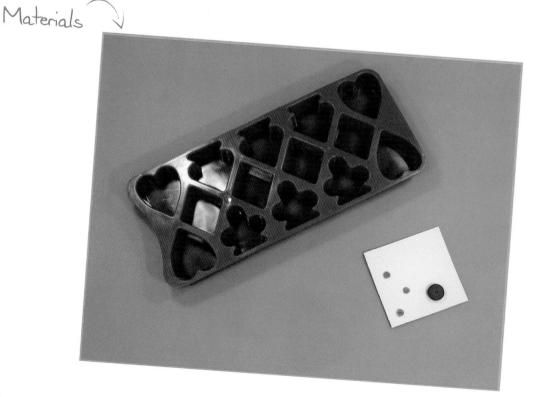

Lidded pots

What you need:

- Concrete mix
- Cardboard mould with lid, 16.5 cm (6½in) in diameter
- Plastic container, 13.5cm (5¼in) in diameter
- Ceramic knob
- Cooking oil and brush
- Drinking straw
- Sand or stones to use as weights
- Sandpaper

What to do:

1. Add water to the concrete mix and pour 1–2cm (½–¾in) of the mixture into the lower cardboard mould. Brush the outside of the plastic container with oil and place in the middle of the concrete; press down gently and weigh down with sand. Then fill the cardboard mould up to the rim of the plastic container with concrete.

2. Leave it to set for several days and then remove the plastic mould carefully.

3. For the lid, first of all make a hole the size of the drinking straw in the middle of the cardboard lid. Push the straw through the hole and stand the lid over a smaller container so that it stands straight.

4. Now stir the concrete mixture again and fill the cardboard lid to a depth of about 2cm (¾in). Leave the concrete to set for several days.

5. Once it has set, remove the concrete lid carefully from the mould, screw the ceramic knob onto it and place the lid on the container.

Materials

Step 4

Pineapple

What you need:

- **Concrete mix**
- **Plastic bottle, 1L (1¾pts), with spotted pattern**
- **Newspaper**
- **Sticky tape**
- **Mottled grey felt, 3mm (⅛in) thick, approx. 16 x 22cm (6¼ x 8¾in)**
- **Hot melt glue and glue gun**
- **Cooking oil and brush**
- **Scissors**
- **Template A (see page 122)**

What to do:

1. Cut off the bottom part of the plastic bottle, just above the start of the neck. Brush the bottle with cooking oil.

2. Make a stopper to place in the pineapple, approximately 3cm (1¼in) in diameter and 11cm (4¼in) high, out of newspaper and sticky tape. This can be removed from the pineapple once set and will create a hollow, making the item less heavy and also provide a hole for sticking in the felt leaves.

3. Add water to the concrete mix and fill the bottle up to about halfway with the mixture. Insert the paper stopper so that about 1–2cm (½–¾in) sticks out above the mould. Fill the mould with concrete up to the rim and leave it to set for several days.

4. Pull the paper stopper out by hand or using a pair of pliers. Cut the mould down the side and remove it.

5. Using Template A, cut eight to ten leaves out of the felt. Arrange these like a leafy stalk in the opening of the concrete shape and glue them in place with hot melt glue.

Step 2

34

Deer and fox figures

What you need:

- Concrete mix
- Sticky-back cover film, approx. 30 x 40cm (11¾ x 15¾in)
- 3 milk cartons or cereal boxes
- Duct tape
- Mottled brown felt, 3mm (⅛in) thick, 10 x 20cm (4 x 7¾in)
- 2 branched twigs
- Waterproof felt-tip pen
- Wooden board, approx. 25 x 35cm (9¾ x 13¾in)
- Cooking oil and brush
- Drill and 4mm (¼in) masonry bit
- General purpose adhesive
- Template B (see page 122)

Step 2

What to do:

1. To make the shapes, stick the sticky-back cover film onto the wooden board. Transfer the figures in Template B onto the covered board using a waterproof felt-tip pen (for the fox, see the dotted line on the template).

2. Cut the milk cartons or cereal boxes into strips approx. 4cm (1½in) wide. Place the strips along the outlines of the motifs and bend them into the shapes of the animals, and then attach them to the wooden board using duct tape. Make sure the shapes are firmly stuck down and no gaps can be seen in between.

3. Add water to the concrete mix, pour into the animal moulds to a depth of about 3cm (1¼in) and leave it to set after several days. After that, take the figures out of the moulds.

4. For the deer, drill two holes into the top of the head as per the template and stick the twigs into these holes. Cut the tails for the deer and the fox out of felt using the template and stick them on.

Concrete & glass vase

What you need:

- **Concrete mix**
- **Glass container, 20cm (7¾in) high, 10cm (4in) in diameter**
- **Plastic bowl, approx. 10cm (4in) high, 13.5cm (5¼in) in diameter**
- **Cooking oil and brush**
- **Brush**
- **Newspaper**
- **Sand or stones to use as weights**
- **Fine-grained sandpaper**

What to do:

1. Brush the inside of the plastic bowl with cooking oil.

2. Add water to the concrete mix and pour the mixture into the bowl to a depth of 1–2cm (½–¾in). Stand the glass container in the middle, pushing it down slightly, and continue to fill the bowl with concrete up to the rim. Shake the bowl gently to release all the air bubbles and to create a flat surface.

3. Line the glass container with newspaper to prevent it getting scratched and weigh it down with sand or stones.

4. Leave the concrete to set for several days. When ready, carefully remove the plastic bowl. Sharp or uneven edges can now be rubbed down with sandpaper.

Step 3

'Water Me' plant pot

What you need:

- **Concrete mix**
- **2 plastic plant pots, approx. 18cm (7in) and 14cm (5½in) in diameter**
- **Grey felt, approx. 5 x 7cm (2 x 2¾in)**
- **Cooking oil and brush**
- **White craft paint**
- **Paint brush**
- **Grey fine-tipped marker pen**
- **Hot melt glue and glue gun**
- **Sand or stones to use as weights**
- **Scissors**

What to do:

1. Brush the inside of the larger plant pot and the outside of the smaller one with oil. Add water to the concrete mix and pour into the larger plant pot up to about halfway with the mixture.

2. Push the smaller plant pot into the middle of the concrete. Weigh it down with sand or stones and leave the concrete to set for several days. When set, separate it from the plant pot moulds.

3. Cut a cloud shape out of the felt and stick it to the concrete pot with hot melt glue. Paint on some small drops of rain and write in the text with a marker pen. Allow everything to dry thoroughly.

Step 2

Step 1

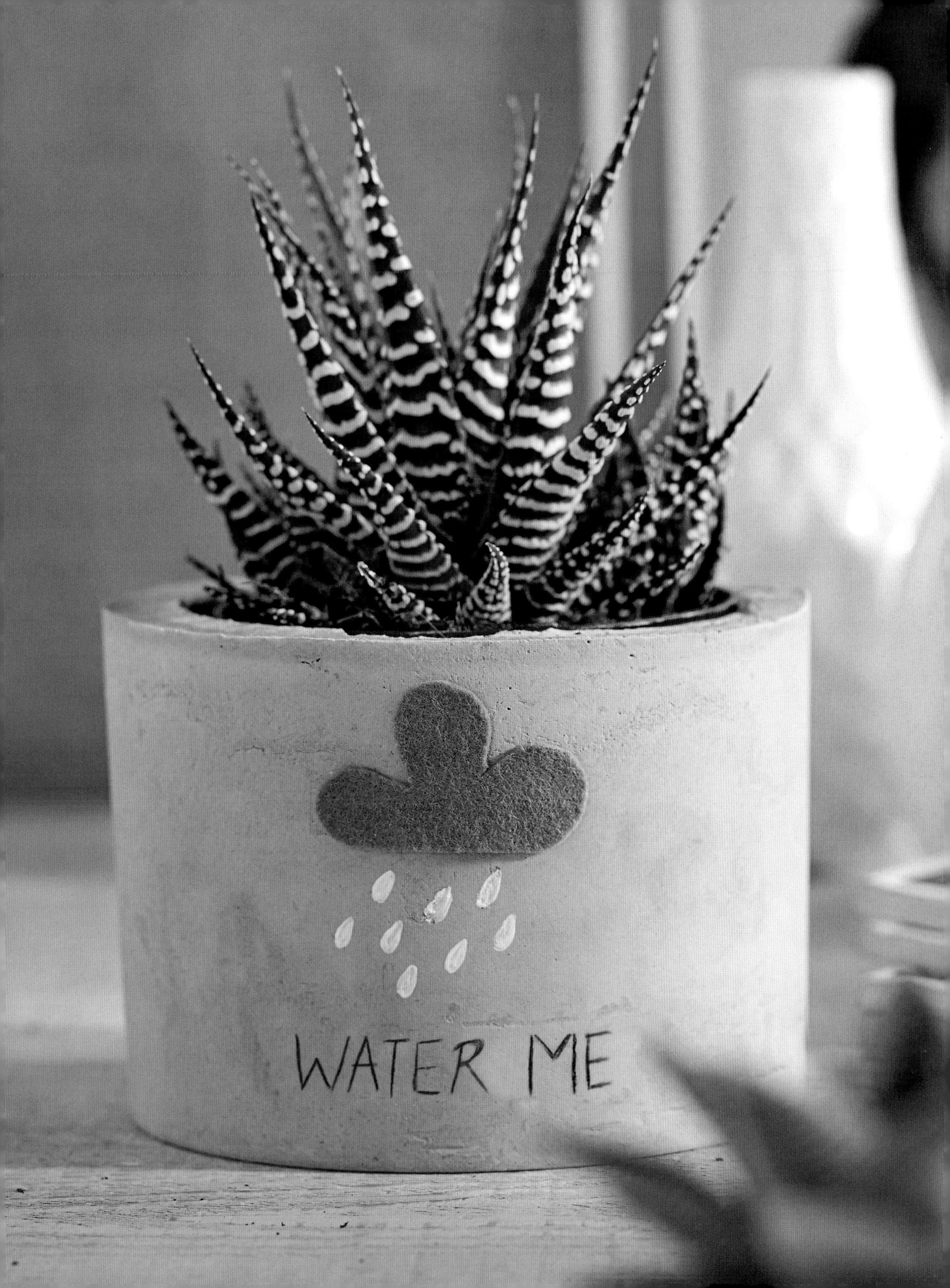
WATER ME

Door stop

What you need:

- **Concrete mix**
- **Plastic bottle, 9cm (3½in) in diameter**
- **Furniture knob with dowel, 4cm (1½in) high**
- **Circle of grey felt, 3mm (⅛in) thick, 9cm (3½in) in diameter**
- **Strip of grey felt, 3mm (⅛in) thick, 30cm (11¾in) long**
- **Iron-on appliqué letters**
- **Hot melt glue and glue gun**
- **Cooking oil and brush**
- **Drill and masonry bit**
- **Needle and thread**

What to do:

1. Cut the plastic bottle down to a height of 13cm (5in) and brush the inside with cooking oil.

2. Add water to the concrete mix and pour the mixture into the bottle up to approx. 1cm (½in) below the rim. Leave the concrete to set for several days, and then remove the plastic mould.

3. Drill a suitably sized hole in the centre of the top of the door stop (bottom of the bottle); insert the dowel and screw in the furniture knob.

4. Stick the circle of felt to the bottom of the door stop with hot melt glue. Iron the iron-on letters onto the strip of felt. Make the strip into a ring by sewing the narrow ends together. Turn the band so the seam is on the inside and pull it over the door stop.

Step 2

'HEY' SIGN

'Hey' sign

What you need:

- **Concrete mix**
- **Letters made of foam, rubber or cardboard, approx. 8cm (3¼in) high**
- **Picture frame, A4 size (297 x 210mm/11.69 x 8.27in)**
- **Plastic-coated placemat, minimum A4 size (297 x 210mm/11.69 x 8.27in)**
- **Cooking oil and brush**
- **General purpose adhesive**
- **Sandpaper**

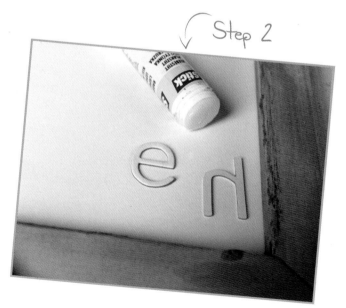

Step 2

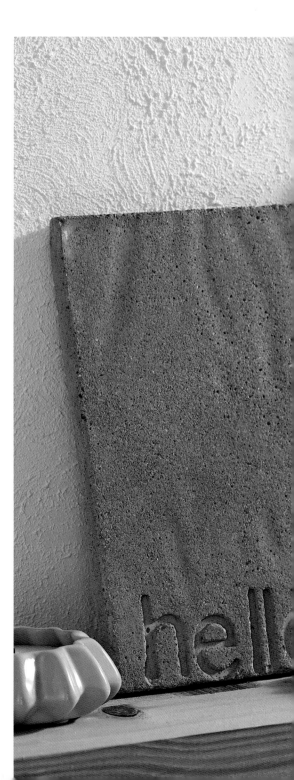

What to do:

1. Make a mould using the picture frame and the placemat, by sticking the frame to the mat.

2. Stick the letters for 'Hey', or another word of your choice, onto the placemat, making sure that it is in reverse. Brush the mould and letters with cooking oil.

3. Add water to the concrete mix and pour the mixture into the mould. Leave the concrete to set for several days. Once it is dry, remove from the mould and rub the edges down with sandpaper, if necessary.

Ombré vases

What you need:

- **Concrete mix**
- **3 tapered wooden moulds, approx. 18cm (7in), 12cm (4¾in) and 9cm (3½in) high**
- **Black, grey and white acrylic paints**
- **Paint brush**
- **3 disposable cups**
- **Cooking oil and brush**
- **Sand or stones to use as weights**

What to do:

1. Brush the wooden moulds with cooking oil. Add water to the concrete mix and pour the mixture into the moulds.

2. Press a disposable cup into the middle of the concrete mixture in each mould and weigh it down with sand or stones. Leave the concrete to set for several days.

3. Lay out the colours for the ombré effect: white, grey and black. Paint stripes onto the vases: black at the bottom, grey in the middle and then white at the top, making sure to leave small gaps in between each shade. Once these stripes have been added and the paint is still fresh, wet a clean brush with water and use this to merge the colours together to produce a gradual progression. You may need to wet your brush several times as you work your way around each vase.

Step 2

Step 3

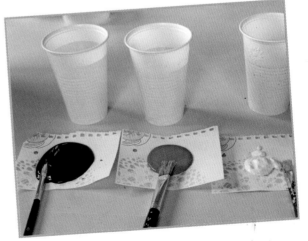

Tiered cake stand

What you need:

- **Concrete mix**
- **2 plastic bowls, 18cm (7in) and 11.5cm (4½in) in diameter**
- **Gold cake stand rod**
- **2 wooden sticks, 5mm (¼in) in diameter and 5cm (2in) long**
- **Cooking oil and brush**
- **Hole punch, 5mm (¼in) diameter holes**
- **Glass and bowl to use as stands**
- **Sandpaper or file**

What to do:

1. Punch a hole in the middle of each plastic bowl with the hole punch, and push a wooden stick through each one to create the hole for the cake stand rod.

2. Brush the insides of the plastic bowls with cooking oil, as well as the wooden sticks. Stand each bowl on a glass or bowl, depending on the size of the plastic bowl, so that the wooden stick remains vertical.

3. Add water to the concrete mix and pour the mixture into the prepared bowls to a depth of about 1.5cm (½in). Leave the bowls to set completely for several days, then remove the moulds and the wooden sticks.

4. Put the cake stand rod through the concrete bowls and screw it together. If the screws supplied are too short, adjust the size of the holes in the concrete plates from underneath using sandpaper or a file.

Step 1

Step 2

48

Pot stands

What you need:

- **Concrete mix**
- **Oval ice cream carton lid, with an edge height of approx. 1.5cm (½in)**
- **Washers, 1–4cm (⅜–1½in) in diameter**
- **Cooking oil and brush**
- **Fine-grained sandpaper**

What to do:

1. Brush the inside of the ice cream carton lid with cooking oil.

2. Add water to the concrete mix and pour the mixture carefully into the mould. Hold the lid on both sides and gently tap the base against your work surface several times to release any air bubbles in the concrete.

3. Place the washers onto the surface of the concrete in your desired pattern, and carefully press them down with your index finger. Tap the base of the lid again several times. Leave the concrete to set for several days.

4. Once it is set, carefully press the concrete out of the lid and rub the edges down with sandpaper.

Materials ⤵

 Step 3

Vases

ROSE

Vase triad

'Rose' vase

What you need:

- Concrete mix
- 3 pieces of foam pipe insulation – 7cm (2¾in) external diameter, 4.5cm (1¾in) internal diameter; 18cm (7in), 22cm (8¾in) and 25cm (9¾in) long
- 3 test tubes, 2.5cm (1in) in diameter, 20cm (7¾in) long
- Cooking oil and brush
- Foil
- Sticky tape

What you need:

- Concrete mix
- Milk carton
- Test tube, 2.5cm (1in) in diameter, 20cm (7¾in) long
- Alphabet stamp set
- Black ink pad
- Cooking oil and brush
- Sticky tape
- Scissors

What to do:

1. Stand the foam tubes on a piece of foil and brush with cooking oil. Add water to the concrete mix and pour the mixture into the tubes up to about halfway.

2. Push the test tubes into the middle of the concrete and fix them in the required position with sticky tape. Fill up the rest of the mould with the concrete.

3. Leave the vases to set for several days then remove the sticky tape and the foam tubes.

What to do:

1. Cut away the top of the milk carton until you are left with a height of 13cm (5in), then brush the inside with cooking oil.

2. Add water to the concrete mix and pour the mixture into the prepared mould up to about half way. Push the test tube into the middle of the concrete and fix in place with sticky tape. Fill up the rest of the mould with the concrete.

3. Leave the concrete to set for several days. When ready, cut away the mould and stamp the name 'Rose' – or another flower – on the side of the vase.

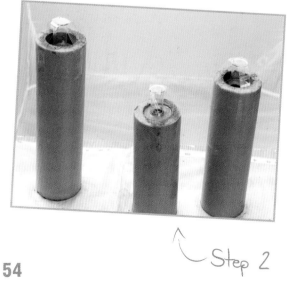

Step 2

Step 2

Round-bellied vase

What you need:

- **Concrete mix**
- **Water container, 5l (1⅓ gal)**
- **Glass bottle with cork, 13.5cm (5¼in) tall**
- **Cooking oil and brush**
- **Plywood board, 18 x 15cm (7 x 6in)**
- **Plywood strip, 6 x 18cm (2½ x 7in)**
- **Sticky tape**

Step 2

What to do:

1. Cut off the lower part of the water container so that the top part measures 13.5cm (5¼in) in height, then brush the inside of the top part, including its screw lid, with cooking oil.

2. Push the cork into the neck of the glass bottle so it is level with the top. Stand the plastic mould with the top facing down in the middle of the plywood board, and then stand the glass bottle upside-down inside it. Place the plywood strip on the bottom of the glass bottle and hold it all together with sticky tape.

3. Add water to the concrete mix and pour the mixture into the mould. Leave the concrete to set for several days.

4. When it is set, take the vase out of the mould and remove the cork from the glass bottle.

Step 3

Soap dish

What you need:

- **Concrete mix**
- **Wall cladding mould**
- **Piece of card**
- **Plasticine**
- **Cooking oil and brush**
- **Sandpaper**

What to do:

1. Decide what size soap dish you want and make a border with plasticine over the negative impression of the wall cladding mould. Strengthen it with card.

2. Brush the plastic areas of the mould with cooking oil. Add water to the concrete mix and pour the mixture into the mould.

3. Leave the concrete to set for several days, then remove the soap dish from the mould. Rub down the uneven areas formed by the plasticine, and any remaining bits of plasticine, using sandpaper.

Step 1

Step 2

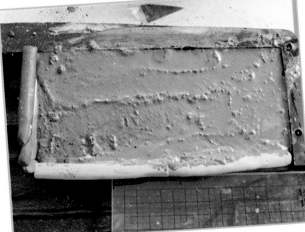

Cake stand

What you need:

- Concrete mix
- Silicone quiche mould, approx. 30cm (11¾in) in diameter
- Ceramic plant pot, approx. 12–15cm (4¾–6in) in diameter
- Cooking oil and brush
- General purpose adhesive

What to do:

1. Brush the inside of the quiche mould with cooking oil.

2. Add water to the concrete mix and pour it into the mould. Gently tap the base of the mould against your work surface to release any air bubbles.

3. Leave the concrete to set for several days, and then remove it from the mould. Put adhesive on the base of the plant pot and stick it to the underside of the cake stand. Allow the adhesive to dry completely.

Tip:

Old wine or water glasses can also be used for the base of the cake stand.

Step 1

'Welcome' sign

What you need:

- Concrete mix
- Rectangular plastic mould, approx. 25 x 10cm (9¾ x 4in)
- Cooking oil and brush
- Neon pink craft paint
- Fine paint brush
- Neon pink decorative cord
- Neon pink beads
- Drinking straw
- Hot melt glue and glue gun
- Scissors
- Screwdriver (optional)

What to do:

1. Cut the drinking straw in half and glue the pieces in two adjacent corners of the plastic mould; these will form the holes to hang the sign from later. Make sure that they are positioned symmetrically.

2. Brush the mould with cooking oil and add water to the concrete mix. Pour the mixture into the mould and leave it to set for several days. Then carefully remove the sign from the mould, along with the drinking straws.

3. Scratch the letters for 'Welcome' into the surface of the sign with the pointed tip of a pair of scissors or a screwdriver. Paint in the engraved words with neon paint using a fine brush.

4. Thread the wooden beads onto the cord and tie a double strand of the cord through the holes to hang the sign.

Step 2

Glittered bowls

What you need:

- **Concrete mix**
- **Plastic bowl, 16cm (6¼in) in diameter, 8cm (3¼in) deep**
- **Plastic bowl, 12cm (4¾in) in diameter, 5cm (2in) deep**
- **Cooking oil and brush**
- **Ivory craft paint**
- **Silver and green glitter paint**
- **Paint brush**
- **Sand or stones to use as weights**

What to do:

1. Brush the inside of the larger plastic bowl and the outside of the smaller bowl with cooking oil.

2. Add water to the concrete mix. Pour the concrete mixture into the larger plastic bowl to a depth of approx. 6cm (2½in). Press the smaller bowl into the middle of the concrete and weigh it down with sand or stones. Leave the concrete to set for several days.

3. Once it is set, remove the moulds and prime the inside of the concrete bowl with ivory craft paint. When the paint is dry, apply several layers of glitter paint, allowing each coat to dry before adding the next.

Materials

Paperweights

What you need:

- **Concrete mix**
- **Various plastic moulds approx. 8 x 6cm (3¼ x 2½in) or approx. 9cm (3½in) in diameter**
- **Cooking oil and brush**
- **Several small objects for making impressions in the concrete**
- **Ribbon**
- **Neon craft paints**
- **Paint brush**
- **Packing tape**
- **Double-sided sticky tape**

What to do:

1. Stick the small objects into the moulds using double-sided sticky tape, and brush everything with plenty of cooking oil.

2. Add water to the concrete mix and pour the mixture into the moulds. Leave it to set for several days. Once it is dry, remove the objects and the moulds.

3. Decorate the sides with neon paint or decorative ribbon.

Tip:

When painting, it is a good idea to use the packing tape to ensure you get clean edges.

Step 3

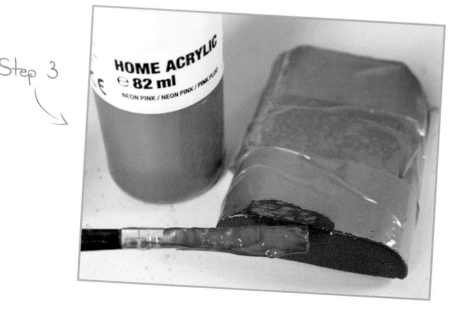

Wine cooler

What you need:

- **Concrete mix**
- **Water container, 5l (1⅓ gal)**
- **Plastic bottle, 9.5cm (3¾in) in diameter, filled with water**
- **Cork, 2.5cm (1in) long**
- **Plywood board, 18 x 15cm (7 x 6in)**
- **Hot melt glue and glue gun**
- **Cooking oil and brush**
- **Packing tape**
- **Scissors**

What to do:

1. Cut the water container down to a height of 22cm (8¾in) and brush the inside with cooking oil.

2. Stick the cork to the bottom of the plastic bottle with hot melt glue, to act as a separator.

3. Add water to the concrete mix and pour the concrete mixture into the water container up to about half way. Stand the plastic bottle in the middle of the concrete. Lay the plywood board on the top of the bottle to hold it straight and attach it to the container with packing tape. Fill in the rest of the mould with concrete.

4. Leave the concrete to set for at least a week, and then remove the mould and the plastic bottle carefully using scissors.

Materials

Drawer knobs

What you need:

- **Concrete mix**
- **Silicone ice cube trays**
- **Screws, approx. 5cm (2in) long**
- **Cooking oil and brush**
- **2 teaspoons**
- **Fine-grained sandpaper**

What to do:

1. Brush the insides of the moulds with cooking oil.

2. Add water to the concrete mix and carefully spoon the mixture into the moulds using two teaspoons. Gently tap the base of the moulds several times to release any air bubbles from the concrete.

3. Press a screw head downwards into the middle of each section of the moulds, making sure that the concrete surface closes around the screw afterwards. Leave the concrete to set for several days.

4. Once it is dry, press the shapes out of the moulds. Finally rub the shapes down with sandpaper to remove any uneven or sharp edges.

Tip:

You can also decorate the drawer knobs by painting them with craft paints.

Step 1

Step 3

Round decorative tile

What you need:

- **Concrete mix**
- **Plant pot saucer, approx. 22cm (8¾in) in diameter**
- **Cooking oil and brush**
- **Black craft paint**
- **Fine paint brush**
- **Soft pencil**
- **Tracing paper (optional)**
- **Access to a computer and printer (optional)**

What to do:

1. Brush the mould with oil and add water to the concrete mix. Pour the mixture into the mould to a depth of about 2.5cm (1in). Leave the concrete to set for several days and then remove it from the mould.

2. Write a saying in pencil in the centre of the concrete tile. Alternatively, type the text in the font you require on the computer, and print it out in reverse to use as a template.

3. Put tracing paper over the template and trace the outline with the soft pencil. Turn the tracing paper over and place it in the centre of the concrete tile. Sharpen your pencil and draw over the lines again. The tracing made in soft pencil will be transferred to the concrete.

4. Finally, paint the text with black craft paint using a fine brush and leave it to dry.

dream
ON
little
DREAMER

Geometric necklaces

What you need:

- **Craft concrete**
- **Modelling foam, 2cm (¾in) thick**
- **Plywood, approx. 4mm (⅛in) thick**
- **Florist wire, 1.6mm (¹⁄₁₆in) in diameter**
- **Gold-coloured texture paste**
- **Silicone caulk**
- **Gold-plated stainless steel wire, approx. 1.2m (47¼in) per chain, 0.38mm (28-gauge) in diameter**
- **Gold-plated crimp friction clasp**
- **Craft knife**
- **Sponge**
- **Masking tape**
- **Jewellery crimpers or superglue**
- **Fine-grained sandpaper**
- **Template C (see page 123)**

Step 2

What to do:

1. Cut the moulds for the square, triangle and rectangle out of the modelling foam with the craft knife, using Template C. To make the holes for the necklace wire, push a piece of florist wire through the 'walls' of each mould, 5mm (¼in) away from the top edge for the square and triangle, and 10mm (½in) away from the edge for the rectangle. Then stick the moulds onto plywood using silicone caulk. For the droplet-shaped mould, cut out a 0.4 x 15cm (¼ x 6in) strip of modelling foam. In the same way as above, push a piece of florist wire horizontally through the droplet mould 'walls' for the necklace wire. Stick the droplet mould onto the plywood board with silicone caulk.

2. Cut small triangles as per the template from a 2cm (¾in) strip of modelling foam. Cut off the patterned surfaces (if there are any on the foam) so that they are smooth and brush them with cooking oil. Place them at different angles within the moulds.

3. Mix the craft concrete and pour it into the moulds. Don't let it completely cover the small triangles. If you wish, you can add more triangles at this point. While the concrete is setting, turn the wires occasionally and carefully pull them out before the concrete is fully set. Once the concrete is dry, remove the moulds and triangles using a craft knife.

4. Stick masking tape onto the concrete shapes to create stripes and any interesting patterns you like. Using the sponge, apply several layers of gold-coloured texture paste to the unmasked areas. Leave until the paint has nearly dried, then pull away the tape before the paint dries fully.

5. Pull several pieces of stainless steel wire through the holes in the concrete shapes. Push the ends of the wire into the crimp fricton clasp and fix in place with crimpers or superglue.

Tealight sconce

What you need:

- **Concrete mix**
- **Rectangular foil baking tray, 18 x 22cm (7 x 8¾in)**
- **Glass container for candle, 8cm (3¼in) high**
- **Cooking oil and brush**
- **Duct tape (optional)**

What to do:

1. Brush the foil tray with cooking oil. Add water to the concrete mix and pour it into the tray, until the mix is just under the rim.

2. Press the glass container into the wet concrete, so that the mixture also runs inside the glass. If necessary, you can hold the glass in the correct position while the concrete sets by pressing duct tape to the glass and walls of the tray.

3. Leave the sconce for several days until it is completely dry, then remove the foil tray and tape.

Step 1

NATURALLY DECORATIVE

Naturally Decorative

Elegant vase candle holder

What you need:

- **Concrete mix**
- **Old, round-bellied ceramic vase**
- **Florist wire, 1.6mm (¹⁄₁₆in) in diameter**
- **Transparent silicone caulk**
- **Gold-plated candle holder to insert in the vase**
- **Cooking oil**
- **Sticky tape**
- **Pin hammer**
- **Fine-grained sandpaper**

What to do:

1. Old ceramic vases are ideal for recycling as moulds. Oil the inside of the vase well, add water to the sieved concrete mix and pour the mixture into the mould. Push a piece of florist wire about 4cm (1½in) into the concrete through the neck of the vase. Fix in place with sticky tape. Turn the wire on a regular basis, so that it does not become stuck. Remove it after about one hour.

2. Leave the concrete to set completely for several days. Once ready, tap the ceramic vase here and there with the pointed tip of the hammer until you have broken away the whole of the old ceramic vase.

3. Rub the concrete vase down with sandpaper. Place the candle holder on top and stick it in place with silicone caulk.

Tips:

- You can avoid ceramic splinters if you place the vase in a transparent rubbish bag before breaking it.

- To add cooking oil to the vase, heat the oil slightly to make it less viscous, pour it into the well (you can use a funnel to make this easier), and turn the vase in your hands so that it runs around the inside.

Floral impression

What you need:

- Concrete mix
- Square mould, 18.5 x 18.5cm (7¼ x 7¼in)
- Dried allium flower heads, 9–11cm (3½–4¼in) in diameter
- White acrylic paint
- Cooking oil and brush
- Scissors
- Fine-grained sandpaper
- Craft knife
- Large sewing needle
- Sponge

What to do:

1. Cut off three dried allium flower heads with stalks and unopened seed pods. Using a pair of scissors, trim the stalks so that the flower heads fit into the mould. Place the stalks together in one corner. Remove the flowers from the mould and split the stalks and seed heads in half, starting from the end of the stalk, so that the stalks and the centre of the spheres form a flat surface.

2. Brush the square mould with cooking oil, add water to the concrete and pour the mixture into the oiled mould. Shake the mould repeatedly to release any air bubbles. Place the allium flower heads into the concrete, with the flat surface facing down. Press the stalks, spherical centres and seed pods half-way down into the concrete mixture.

3. Once the surface is dry, carefully lift out the allium flower heads. The thin stalks of the seed pods can be further scratched out with a craft knife. Leave the concrete to set for several days. Once it is ready, remove it from the mould and rub down the concrete imprint with fine-grained sandpaper. Extract any plant remnants from the indentations with a needle. Use a sponge to dab a little white paint on the flower heads.

Cactus

CACTUS

What you need:

- **Concrete mix**
- **Modelling foam**
- **Wooden board, 24 x 30cm (9½ x 11¾in)**
- **Sticky-back cover film, 24 x 30cm (9½ x 11¾in)**
- **Green colouring pigment**
- **Balls of cork – 1 x 20mm (¾in) and 2 x 25mm (1¼in) in diameter**
- **Plant pot suitable for repotting**
- **Freezer bag**
- **Craft knife**
- **Template D (see page 123)**

What to do:

1. Transfer Template D onto paper, cut it out and lay it on the modelling foam. Cut the outline of the cactus with the craft knife and remove the inner section to create the mould.

2. Cover the wooden board with sticky-back cover film. Stick the modelling foam mould on the board.

3. Colour the water that you'll use to make the concrete using the green colouring pigment. When it''s the correct colour, stir it into the concrete mix. Pour the concrete mixture into the mould and leave to set for a couple of hours.

4. Press the balls of cork half-way into the concrete, once it has hardened a little. Leave everything to set for two days. Take the cactus out of the mould.

5. Line the plant pot with the freezer bag. Mix up a small amount of concrete, pour it into the plant pot until it is half full and leave to set. Place the cactus in the pot, prop it up from the side and fill up the plant pot with freshly mixed concrete. Leave to set for two more days. Once the concrete is ready, remove the freezer bag or cut it off at the top edge using the craft knife.

Stylish embroidered necklace

What you need:

- **Craft concrete**
- **Gold-plated cabochon setting, 2.5cm (1in) in diameter**
- **Beaded necklace chain, 2mm (1/16in) in diameter and 1m (39½in) long**
- **Sewing needle**
- **Black embroidery thread**
- **Pencil**
- **Drill with masonry bit, 2mm (1/16in) in diameter**

What to do:

1. Add water to a small quantity of craft concrete and pour it into the cabochon setting. Leave until completely dry.

2. Mark the position of the holes for the embroidery design with a pencil. Carefully drill holes through the concrete and the cabochon setting; avoid applying too much pressure to prevent the holes from crumbling.

3. Embroider the motif as shown in the photograph. Secure the beginning and end of the thread with knots on the reverse side of the setting.

Materials

Lampshade

LAMPSHADE

What you need:

- **Lampshade with suitable light fitting, 13.5cm (5¼in) in diameter, 30cm (11¾in) tall**
- **Concrete effect paste**
- **Concrete glaze kit**
- **Sanding sponge**
- **Sewing needle**
- **Drilling awl**
- **Brush**
- **Template E (see page 123)**

What to do:

1. Transfer the pattern from Template E onto the lampshade. Prick dots through the fabric, and expand them to the required size with the drilling awl.

2. Apply a thin layer of concrete effect paste, following the manufacturer's instructions. Once it is dry, apply a thicker layer. Before the second layer of paste is completely dry, prick through the holes once again to prevent them from closing over.

3. Once it is dry, rub the surface down with the sanding sponge, and then use the sponge to apply the dark concrete glaze. When this is dry, wipe a layer of the light concrete glaze over the top.

4. Attach the light fitting following the manufacturer's instructions and hang the lampshade.

Foxes

Foxes

What you need:

- Concrete mix
- Modelling foam
- Wide sticky tape
- Grey cardboard
- Solvent-free adhesive
- Ruler
- Pencil
- Paper
- Craft knife
- Sandpaper
- White acrylic paint
- Paint brush
- Template F (see page 124)

Step 2

What to do:

1. Transfer both F templates to a piece of paper and cut them out. For each template, cut out two pieces of modelling foam measuring 23 x 38cm (9 x 15in). Lay the template onto one of the modelling foam pieces and cut the outline with the craft knife. Hold the craft knife vertically so that the cut edges do not slant. Remove the inner sections – but don't throw them away. Close the bottom edge of the moulds by sticking a strip of grey cardboard onto it, then stick the mould onto the second piece of modelling foam.

2. With the inner sections, carve out symmetrical, angular shapes with the craft knife to create interesting slanted surfaces on your foxes. Bear in mind that what you cut into the mould will be the mirror image of the finished animal figure.

3. Place the trimmed inner sections back into their corresponding moulds and glue them in place. Cover any joint lines on the underneath of the mould with sticky tape, if necessary.

4. Mix up the concrete according to the instructions and pour it into the mould. Leave it to set for one or two days. Take the figures out of the moulds and rub down the surfaces with sandpaper. Glaze some of the surfaces with watered-down acrylic paint.

Step 3

Bowl with side plate

What you need:

- **Concrete mix**
- **Modelling foam, 5cm (2in) thick**
- **Plywood, approx. 4mm (⅛in) thick**
- **2 plastic hemispheres, 14 and 16cm (5½ and 6¼in) in diameter**
- **Cooking oil and brush**
- **Transparent silicone caulk**
- **White acrylic marker pen, 2–4mm (¹⁄₁₆–⅛in) nib**
- **Turquoise acrylic paint**
- **Paint brush**
- **Duct tape**
- **Scroll saw with fine blade, hot wire foam cutter or craft knife**
- **Sandpaper**
- **Cup**
- **Template G (see pages 124 and 125)**

What to do:

1. Cut the mould out of modelling foam using Template G. If you are using a scroll saw, push the saw blade with the serrated edge facing downwards into the modelling foam, clamp it and saw. Rub the mould down with sandpaper if necessary. Coat the base with silicone caulk and stick it onto the plywood; you can tape it down with duct tape as well, if need be.

2. Brush the outside of the larger of the two hemispheres with oil. Add water to the concrete mixture and pour it into the mould until the mix is approx. 2.5cm (1in) from the rim. Gently press the oiled hemisphere into the concrete at one end of the mould. Weigh it down with stones to make an impression measuring 11cm (4¼in) in diameter. Leave the concrete to set for several days. Once dry, take out the hemisphere and remove the concrete item from the mould. Sand down any rough surfaces with sandpaper.

3. Using the two hemispheres, make a round bowl: brush the inside of the larger hemisphere with oil. Stand it on a cup or something similar. Pour in some freshly made concrete into the mould up to about half way. Brush the outside of the smaller hemisphere with oil and press it into the middle of the concrete until the mixture reaches the rim of the larger hemisphere – add more concrete at this point if necessary. Leave to set for several days.

4. Once it is dry, remove the bowl and paint the inside with watered-down turquoise paint. Draw white lines and circles onto the plate with the acrylic marker pen. Paint some areas pale turquoise, using watered-down paint in some parts, as desired. Leave to dry completely.

Tip:

If you would like to make these items extra-safe for food use, you can paint your items with porcelain paint instead and add a sealer. To do this, let your concrete and paint fully set, then apply either a wax (such as carnauba or bees) with a cloth, a penetrating repellant sealer or urethanes topical sealer.

Step 3

Flower picture

What you need:

- **Concrete mix**
- **2 empty kitchen rolls**
- **Cooking oil and brush**
- **Apricot craft paint**
- **Paint brush**
- **Black fine-tipped marker pen**
- **Picture frame, A3 size (297 x 420 mm/11.7 x 16.5in)**
- **White card, 160gsm (60lbs)**
- **Hot melt glue and glue gun**
- **Pencil**
- **Scissors**
- **Coin**
- **Old flat plate or tray, A3 size (297 x 420 mm/11¾ x 16½in)**

What to do:

1. Flatten the kitchen rolls, cut them into four or five pieces and bend them into the shape of leaves. Lay the leaf moulds onto an old, flat plate or tray that has been brushed in oil.

2. Mix up the concrete and pour it into the moulds to a depth of around 5mm (¼in). Leave the concrete to set for several days, and then remove the cardboard.

3. Cut the white card to fit the picture frame. Draw three flower stems of different lengths with the black marker pen. Create flower blossoms by drawing around a coin with a pencil and painting in the circles with apricot craft paint.

4. Arrange the concrete leaves in pairs along the flower stems and stick them in place with hot melt glue. Finally, put the finished picture into the frame, excluding the glass.

Step 1

Together forever intials

What you need:

- **Concrete mix**
- **Modelling foam, 5cm (2in) thick**
- **Plywood, approx. 4mm (⅛in) thick**
- **Transparent silicone caulk**
- **White acrylic paint marker, 2–4mm (1/16–⅛in) in diameter**
- **Duct tape**
- **Aluminium foil**
- **Cooking oil and brush**
- **Sandpaper**
- **Cut-resistant mat**
- **Letter stencils (optional)**
- **Craft knife**
- **Access to computer and printer (optional)**
- **Rubber spatula**
- **Template H (see page 125)**

What to do:

1. Saw or cut the letters out of modelling foam, following the pattern in Template H – pay particular attention to the join. If other letters are required, arrange the letters on the computer using a simple font and print them out as a template.

2. Rub down the surfaces with sandpaper. Stick the letters in reverse to the plywood with silicone caulk, removing any extra bits of caulk with the spatula. Brush the mould with oil and secure it to the board with duct tape.

3. On a cut-resistant mat, cut an '&' in the foil using the craft knife, freehand or with a stencil if necessary. Mix up the concrete and pour it into the mould. Press the '&' into the concrete mixture in the join between the letters, making sure that the surface is above the mixture by approx. 1mm (1/32in).

4. Leave the concrete to set for several days. When ready, bend the plywood board to lift off the mould and the filling. Remove the mould and the foil stencil. Rub down the surfaces and edges with sandpaper and colour the '&' symbol white with the paint marker.

Step 2

94

Splattered bottle vases

What you need:

- **Different-shaped bottles**
- **Concrete effect paste**
- **Concrete glaze kit**
- **Copper and turquoise acrylic paints**
- **Paint brush**
- **Toothpick or cocktail stick**

What to do:

1. Mix up the concrete effect paste as instructed on the packet and spread a thin, bonding layer of it on the bottles. Leave it to dry. Apply a second thicker layer and once again leave it to dry.

2. Paint the bottles with the glaze following the manufacturer's instructions, then stand or lie the bottles as required to make the paint run in the desired direction. Apply a generous coat of acrylic paint using the brush. The paint should not be thin and should drip down slowly.

3. Use the toothpick or cocktail stick to carefully pull the drips a little bit away from the paint surface; this will control the direction somewhat. Leave the paint to dry.

EASTERN

Eastern Inspired

Decorative leaf plate

What you need:

- **Concrete mix**
- **Square mould, 25 x 25cm (9¾ x 9¾in)**
- **Gilding size**
- **Deco gilding flakes, gold**
- **Black marker pen (optional)**
- **Cut-resistant mat**
- **Craft knife**
- **Aluminium foil**
- **Sticky tape**
- **Cooking oil and brush**
- **Paint brush**
- **Fine-grained sandpaper**
- **Ruler (optional)**
- **Template I (see page 126)**

What to do:

1. On a cut-resistant mat, use the craft knife to cut out the shapes shown in Template I from foil. Attach the template underneath the foil with sticky tape to strengthen it.

2. Brush the square mould with cooking oil. Mix up the concrete so that it is not too runny and pour it into the oiled mould. Place the foil stencil on the smooth surface of the concrete; gently press the solid section of the stencil repeatedly into the concrete with the paint brush, so that the concrete rises up about 1mm (¹⁄₃₂in) above the foil in the cut-out sections. Leave to set for several days.

3. Once the concrete is dry, lift off the foil and take the plate out of the mould. Rub it down with sandpaper if necessary. Brush gilding size onto a few of the raised bars of the leaves and leave it to dry. Gently press some of the gilding flakes onto it with the handle of your brush and then sweep away any protruding concrete with a dry brush. Draw lines around the gold areas with the black marker and ruler if desired.

Step 2

Textured vase

What you need:

- **Concrete mix**
- **Modelling foam, 5cm (2in) thick**
- **Plywood, approx. 4mm (⅛in) thick**
- **Grey plastic pipe, approx. 2cm (¾in) in diameter**
- **Transparent silicone caulk**
- **Test tube, 1.5cm (½in) in diameter**
- **Craft knife**
- **Scroll saw with fine blade (optional)**
- **Duct tape**
- **Cooking oil and brush**
- **Aluminium foil**
- **Cut-resistant mat**
- **Fine-grained sandpaper**
- **Template J (see page 126)**

What to do:

1. Cut the mould out of the modelling foam using Template J. If you are using a scroll saw, cut a hole with the craft knife in the middle of the cut-out section, insert the saw blade with the serrated edge facing downwards, clamp it and cut out the central section; once you have finished sawing, loosen the blade and remove it. Stick the mould onto the plywood with silicone caulk and secure with duct tape.

2. Push the piece of plastic pipe through the top wall of the mould, right into the middle of the cut-out section, to create a hole to insert the test tube. Push the test tube into the hole and tape over the opening with duct tape to hold it in place.

3. On a cut-resistant surface, use the craft knife to cut out the stencil from foil. Attach the template underneath the foil with sticky tape to strengthen it.

4. Mix up the concrete so that it is not too runny and pour it into the mould. Place the foil stencil on the smooth concrete surface so that it is slightly off-centre and sits around the lower-left edge of the mould. Gently press the solid sections of the stencil repeatedly into the concrete with the handle of your brush, until the concrete rises about 1mm (¹⁄₃₂in) above the foil in the cut-out sections.

5. Leave the concrete to set for several days. When it has set, remove the stencil and take the concrete item out of the mould. Rub down the vase with sandpaper.

Step 4

Raindrop mobile

What you need:

- **Concrete mix**
- **Thin cardboard**
- **Flat old plate or tray**
- **Cooking oil and brush**
- **Apricot, turquoise and white craft paints**
- **Paint brush**
- **Turquoise glitter**
- **Wooden rod, approx. 30cm (11¾in)**
- **String or twine**
- **Strong sticky tape**
- **Hot melt glue and glue gun**
- **Craft knife**
- **Sticky tape**
- **Masking tape**

What to do:

1. Cut five strips of cardboard measuring 28 x 2cm (11 x ¾in), and make droplets out of the strips by sticking the ends together with sticky tape on the outside. Lay the moulds on a flat old plate or tray which has been brushed with oil.

2. Mix up the concrete. Pour it into the moulds to a depth of about 5mm (¼in). Leave the droplets to set for several days and then remove them from the moulds.

3. Stick masking tape in diagonal stripes onto each droplet. Paint one apricot stripe and one white on each. Leave to dry. Remove the masking tape. Finally, paint on the turquoise stripes and sprinkle glitter over the wet paint. Leave to dry.

4. Cut five pieces of string or twine into different lengths. Stick one end of each piece of twine to the back of a droplet with hot melt glue. Once dry, tie the other end of the twine to the wooden rod, keeping an equal distance between the threads. Attach a long length of twine to each of the end droplet knots to hang up the mobile.

Step 1

Step 3

Smartphone cushion

What you need:

- **Concrete mix**
- **2l (3½pt) freezer bag, 20 x 31cm (7¾ x 12¼in)**
- **White and turquoise acrylic paints**
- **Paint brush**
- **Black fine-tipped marker pen**
- **Sticky tape**
- **Foil heat sealer, or bowl of water**
- **Foldback/binder clip (optional)**
- **Smartphone, or similar**
- **Hardback book**
- **Fine-grained sandpaper**
- **Support, e.g. plywood board**

What to do:

1. Stand an old hardback book slightly open with the spine facing upwards. Wrap it in sticky tape and stick it to a support (here a plywood board is used).

2. Mix up the concrete and pour it into a 2l (3½pt) freezer bag. Keep the top edges clean. When the bag is filled to a depth of 10cm (4in), close the opening. You need to make sure that the air is completely removed from the upper half of the bag. To do this, you can use a foil heat sealer. Alternatively, reopen a small section of the freezer bag, dip the bag in a bowl of water – take care not to get any water near the opening – and this will create a vacuum. Close the bag once more, and secure with a foldback/binder clip if necessary. This creates a 20cm (7¾in) square 'cushion'.

3. Attach the flat top of the freezer bag to the book cover with sticky tape; approx. one-third of the cushion should be left lying on the horizontal surface.

4. Wrap a smartphone (or something of a similar shape and weight, like a calculator) in a thin plastic bag and press it into the concrete cushion so that it is well embedded, and until the outer layer of the concrete takes on the overall shape of the phone. Leave to set for several days.

5. Once the concrete is set, remove the bag and sand down the concrete cushion. Paint small white and turquoise squares on the cushion and outline some of the squares in black.

Step 4

Fruit

What you need:

- **Concrete mix**
- **Balloons**
- **2 wooden bead hemispheres, 2cm (¾in) in diameter**
- **Small funnel**
- **Scissors**
- **Sticky tape**
- **Binding wire or string**
- **Books**
- **Twigs**
- **Superglue**

What to do:

1. For the apple, mix up the concrete and pour it into a balloon using the funnel. Tie up the balloon securely above the curve using wire or string. Cut off the remaining thin neck of the balloon.

2. To create the contours of the apple, lay about 20cm (7¾in) of sticky tape in strips on the table, with the sticky side upwards; put a wooden bead hemisphere with the flat side facing down in the middle of the sticky tape and place the balloon filled with concrete on top of it. Put the second wood bead hemisphere, with the rounded side facing down, on the top of the balloon. Stick strips of tape up over the upper bead hemisphere from the right- and left-hand sides of the balloon. Finally, weigh down the 'apple' with books to create the oval shape of the apple. Leave to set for a few days.

3. Once the concrete is set, remove the bead hemispheres, cut the balloon and remove it from the concrete item. Sand down the apple with sandpaper and glue a piece of twig in the upper hollow to represent the stalk.

4. To make the pear, fill the balloon completely with concrete mixture and tie it higher up the neck. Stand the base of the balloon on a wood bead hemisphere and secure in place with tape. Leave to set, and finish off in the same way as the apple.

Step 4

Hummingbird clock

What you need:

- **Concrete mix**
- **Modelling foam**
- **Square mould, 25 x 25cm, (9¾ x 9¾in)**
- **Wooden rod, 1cm (½in) in diameter, 4cm (1½in) long**
- **Quartz clock mechanism with 1cm (⅜in) shaft**
- **Clock hands, 7 x 9cm (2¾ x 3½in)**
- **Self-adhesive cork sheet**
- **Cooking oil and brush**
- **Craft knife**
- **General purpose adhesive**
- **Pliers**
- **Template K (see page 126)**

What to do:

1. Cut four triangles out of modelling foam using Template K and stick them into each corner of the square mould.

2. Glue the wooden rod in the middle of the base of the mould to form the hole for the spindle of the clock mechanism. Once dry, brush the rod with cooking oil.

3. Mix up the concrete following the instructions and pour it into the mould to a depth of 1cm (½in). Leave it to set for one or two days. When it is dry, carefully pull out the wooden rod with a pair of pliers. Take the concrete object out of the mould and insert the clock mechanism.

4. Transfer the motifs to the cork (using the template as a pattern), cut them out, remove the backing and stick them onto the clock face.

Artfully Jagged

Geometric jewellery bowl

What you need:

- Concrete mix
- Modelling foam, 2cm (¾in) thick
- Plywood, approx. 4mm (⅛in) thick
- Plastic hemisphere, 10cm (4in) in diameter
- Silicone caulk
- Craft knife
- Scroll saw with fine blade (optional)
- Fine-grained sandpaper
- Cooking oil and brush
- Rough sponge
- Stones to use as weights
- Black and white acrylic paints (optional)
- Paint brush (optional)
- Template L (see page 127)

What to do:

1. Cut three star-shaped moulds out of modelling foam using Template L with a scroll saw or craft knife. If you are using a saw, cut a hole in the middle with the craft knife, insert the saw blade with the serrated edge facing downwards, and clamp it. Once you have finished cutting, loosen the blade and remove it. Rub down the moulds with fine-grained sandpaper, if necessary, to give the cut edges of the foam a smooth surface.

2. Place the three moulds on top of each other at different angles and stick them together with silicone caulk. Stick the bottom layer to the plywood. Mix up the concrete and pour it into the mould up to about three-quarters of the way up.

3. Brush the outside of the plastic hemisphere with oil and gently press it into the middle of the surface of the concrete. Weigh it down with stones. Fill in the rest of the mould with concrete if necessary, and leave to set for several days.

4. Once the concrete is set, take out the hemisphere and remove the mould. Bend the plywood board gently to release the base layer.

5. Rub down the bowl with sandpaper and clean it with a rough sponge. You can paint the corners of the bowl in black and white if you wish.

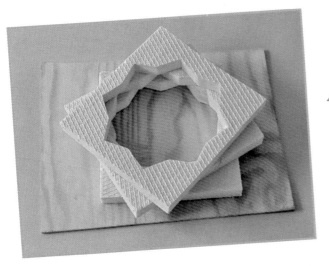

Step 2

Geometric vase

What you need:

- **Concrete mix**
- **Modelling foam, 2cm (¾in) thick**
- **Plywood, approx. 4mm (⅛in) thick**
- **Silicone caulk**
- **Test tube, 15.5cm (6¼in), 16mm (⅝in) in diameter**
- **Craft knife**
- **Scroll saw with fine blade (optional)**
- **Fine-grained sandpaper**
- **Small stones or round rod to use as weights**
- **Template M (see page 127)**

What to do:

1. Cut out a square from eight layers of modelling foam using Template M with a scroll saw or craft knife. As you did for the jewellery bowl, place these on top of each other at angles and stick them together with silicone caulk. Stick your foam 'tower' onto the plywood for the base.

2. Fill the mould with concrete until you are 2.5cm (1in) short of the top of the mould. Push the test tube into the middle of the concrete up to its rim and fill it with small stones, or press it down with a round rod.

3. Leave the concrete to set fo several days. Once the concrete is set, take the object out of the mould and rub down any uneven areas with sandpaper.

Step 2

Woven-style basket and tray

What you need:

- **Concrete mix**
- **Modelling foam**
- **Oval woven basket, approx. 27 x 13cm (10¾ x 5in)**
- **Square woven basket, base measuring 20 x 20cm (7¾ x 7¾in)**
- **Square mould, 25 x 25cm (9¾ x 9¾in)**
- **Silicone caulk**
- **Craft knife**
- **Scroll saw with fine blade or hot wire cutter (optional)**
- **Cooking oil and brush**
- **Fine-grained sandpaper**
- **Sticky tape**
- **Stones to use as weights**

What to do:

1. For the basket, seal the holes on the outside by brushing them with silicone caulk. Leave to dry, according to the manufacturer's instructions.

2. To make the deep interior of the oval basket, cut an impression out of modelling foam based on the measurements of the basket, using a scroll saw, hot wire cutter or craft knife. Once you have the main shape, and using the craft knife, cut or taper the sides of the impression to fit inside the basket, leaving a 1.5cm (¾in) gap all around.

3. Brush the inside of the basket with oil. Mix up the concrete and pour it into the basket up to about half way. Press the modelling foam impression into the concrete mixture and fix it in place with sticky tape. Fill in the rest of the mould with concrete if necessary.

4. Once the concrete is set, take the concrete basket out of the mould. Rub down any sharp edges with sandpaper.

5. For the tray, seal the holes on the inside of the square basket with silicone caulk, as you did for the basket in step 1. Brush the square mould with oil.

6. Make up the concrete mix and pour it into the mould to a depth of about 3cm (1¼in). Press the square basket into the middle of the concrete mixture and weigh it down with stones.

7. After about two hours carefully remove the basket and leave the concrete to set for several days. Once set, remove the tray from the mould.

Step 2

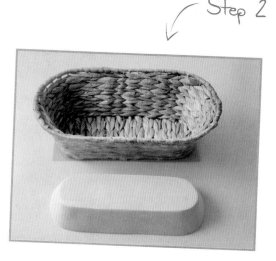

Step 5

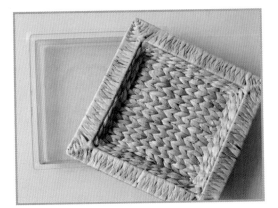

114

Minimalist diamond necklace

What you need:

- **Craft concrete**
- **Diamond-shaped mould, 2.9 x 3.9cm (1⅛ x 1½in)**
- **Gold-plated crimp bead, 2.5mm (⅛in) in diameter**
- **Gold-plated stainless steel wire, 0.38mm (28-gauge) in diameter, approx. 1m (39½in) long**
- **Platinum-plated stainless steel wire, 0.38mm (28-gauge) in diameter, approx. 40cm (15¾in) long**
- **Gold-plated spacer ring, open, 12mm (28-gauge) in diameter**
- **Platinum-plated crimp friction clasp**
- **Small flat-nose pliers**
- **Drill with masonry bit (optional)**

What to do:

1. Pull about 60cm (23½in) of gold-plated wire a total of six times through a crimp bead and arrange the wire in gradually increasing circles at an equal distance from each other. Finally, press the crimp bead with the pliers to secure the wire circles and cut off any excess wire.

2. Mix up the craft concrete and pour it into the diamond-shaped mould. Make sure you don't cover the hole former. Press the crimp bead that is securing the wire circles into the concrete. Push down on the wire circles so that the crimp bead remains underneath the surface of the concrete. Once the concrete is set, take the whole shape out of the mould.

3. Insert a spacer ring in the hole at the top of concrete diamond. Pull one gold- and one platinum-coloured wire through the ring. Insert the ends of the wires into the crimp friction clasp and squeeze the ends of the clasp together with the pliers to secure them.

Tip:

If your mould doesn't have a hole former, drill a small hole into the upper corner of the diamond shape once the craft concrete has set.

Step 2

Elegant leaf dishes

What you need:

- **Concrete mix**
- **Modelling foam**
- **Plywood, approx. 4mm (⅛in) thick**
- **Transparent silicone caulk**
- **Glass-effect gel**
- **Plastic tray, 29 x 14cm (11½ x 5½in)**
- **Cooking oil and brush**
- **Fine-grained sandpaper**
- **Scroll saw with fine blade, hot wire cutter or craft knife**
- **Sticky tape**
- **Templates N and O (see page 127)**

What to do:

1. For the leaf-shaped dish, cut a leaf-like mould out of modelling foam using the large leaf in Template N with either a scroll saw, hot wire cutter or craft knife. For the deep interior of the dish, cut out a smaller leaf shape using the small leaf in Template N. Sand down any rough edges on the foam with sandpaper.

2. Stick the base of the larger mould to the plywood with silicone caulk. Brush the inside of the mould with cooking oil.

3. Make up the concrete mix and pour it into the mould up to about half way. Brush the smaller leaf shape with oil, press it into the concrete mixture and fix it in place with sticky tape. Fill in the rest of the mould with concrete if necessary.

4. Leave to set for several days. Once it is set, take the object out of the mould and rub it down with sandpaper.

5. For the flat dish with leaf motifs, cut two leaf shapes out of modelling foam using Template O with either a scroll saw, hot wire cutter of craft knife. Sand down any rough edges with sandpaper. Dot bead-like balls of glass-effect gel on the underside of the leaf shapes and leave them to dry.

6. Brush the plastic tray with oil, fill it with prepared concrete mixture and then press the leaf shapes into the concrete, approx. 1cm (½in) deep. Fix them in place with sticky tape.

7. Remove the dish from the mould when the concrete is set.

Step 1

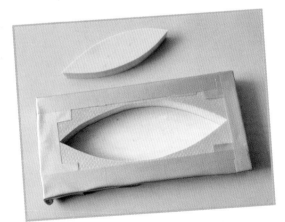

Step 5

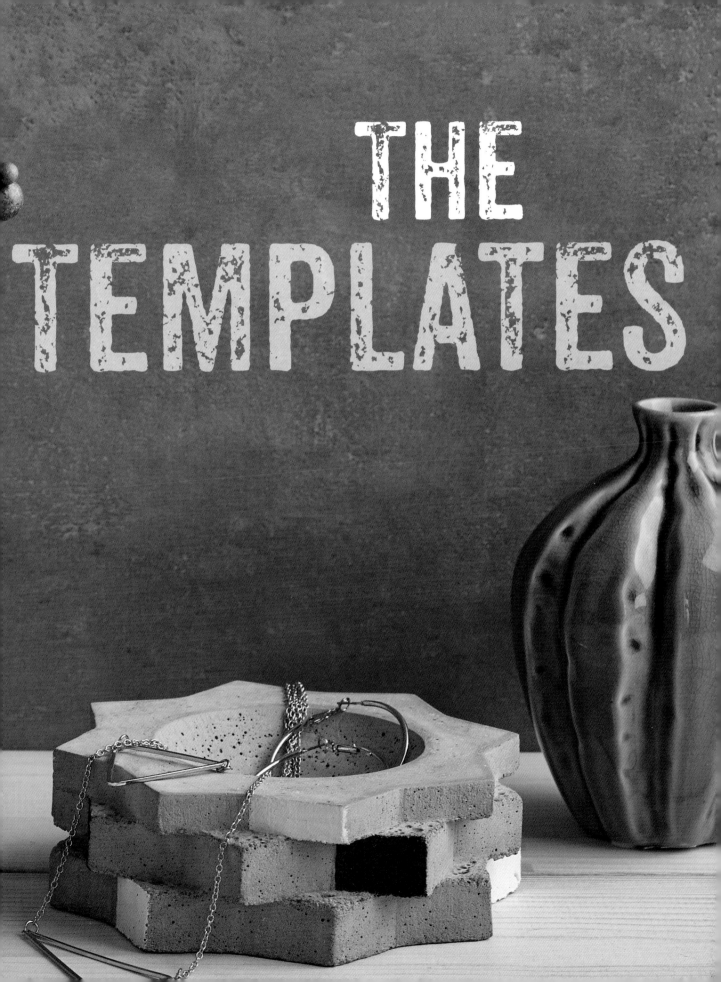

THE TEMPLATES

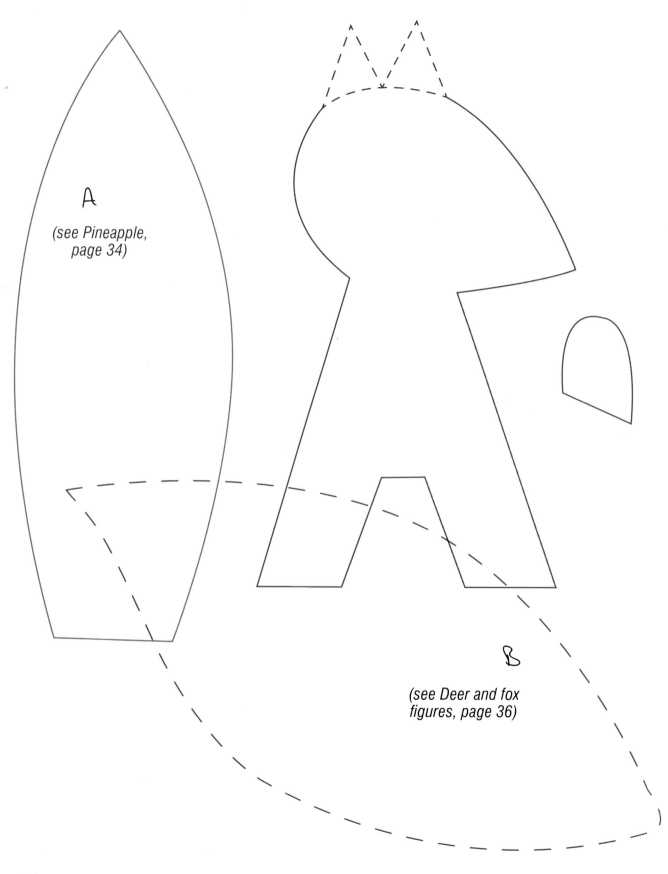

A

*(see Pineapple,
page 34)*

B

*(see Deer and fox
figures, page 36)*

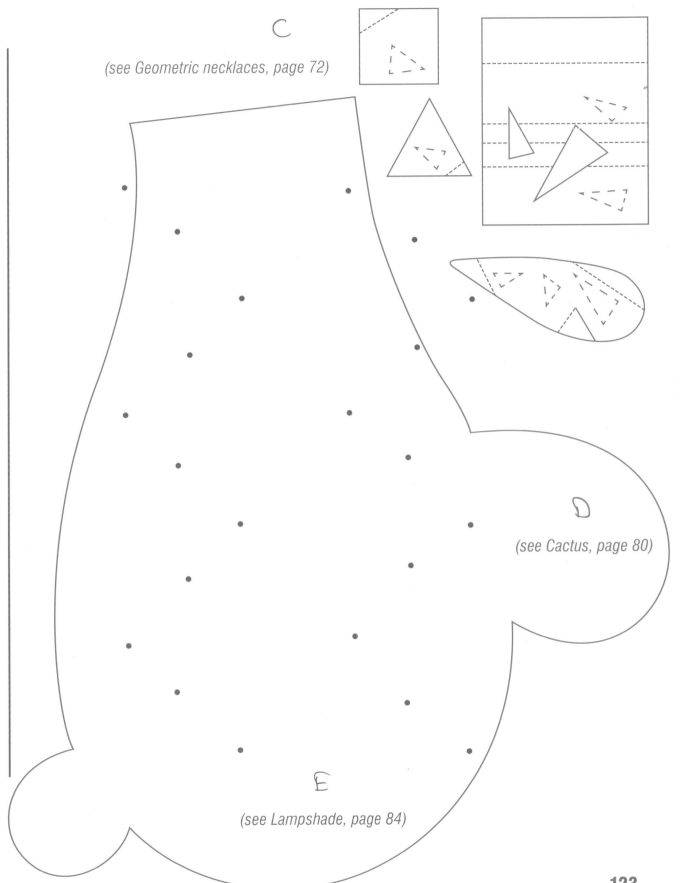

C

(see Geometric necklaces, page 72)

D

(see Cactus, page 80)

E

(see Lampshade, page 84)

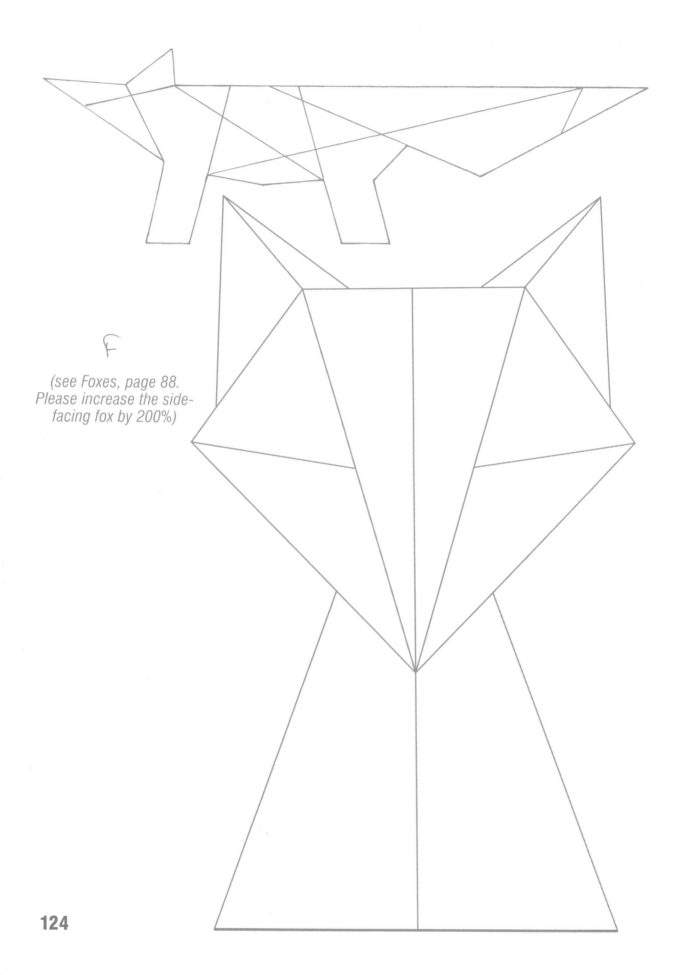

F

*(see Foxes, page 88.
Please increase the side-
facing fox by 200%)*

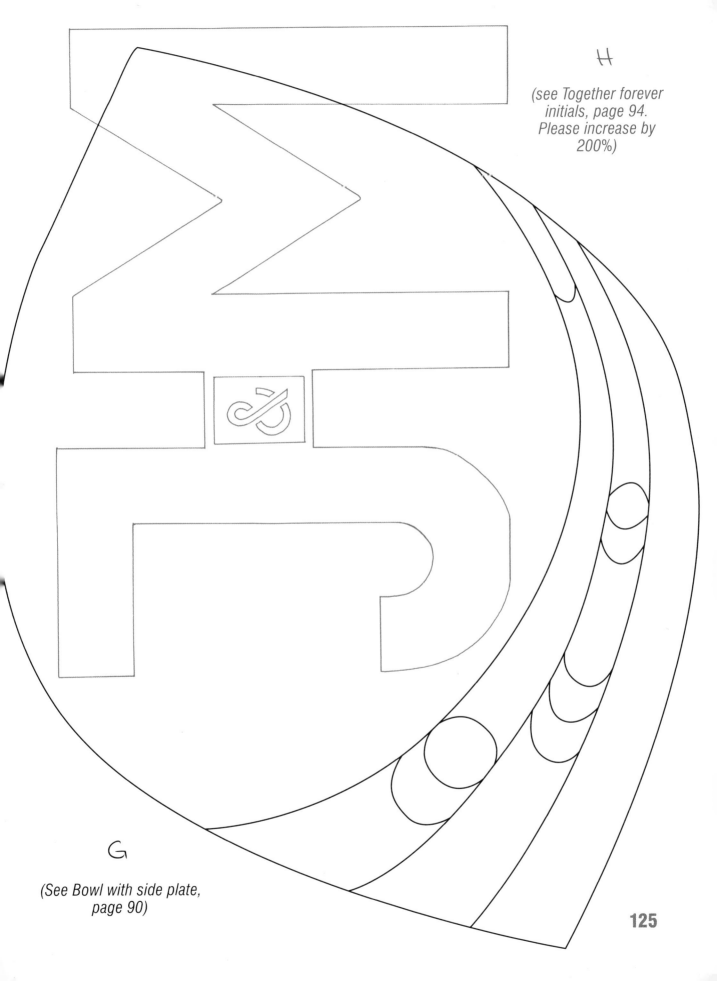

H

*(see Together forever
initials, page 94.
Please increase by
200%)*

G

*(See Bowl with side plate,
page 90)*

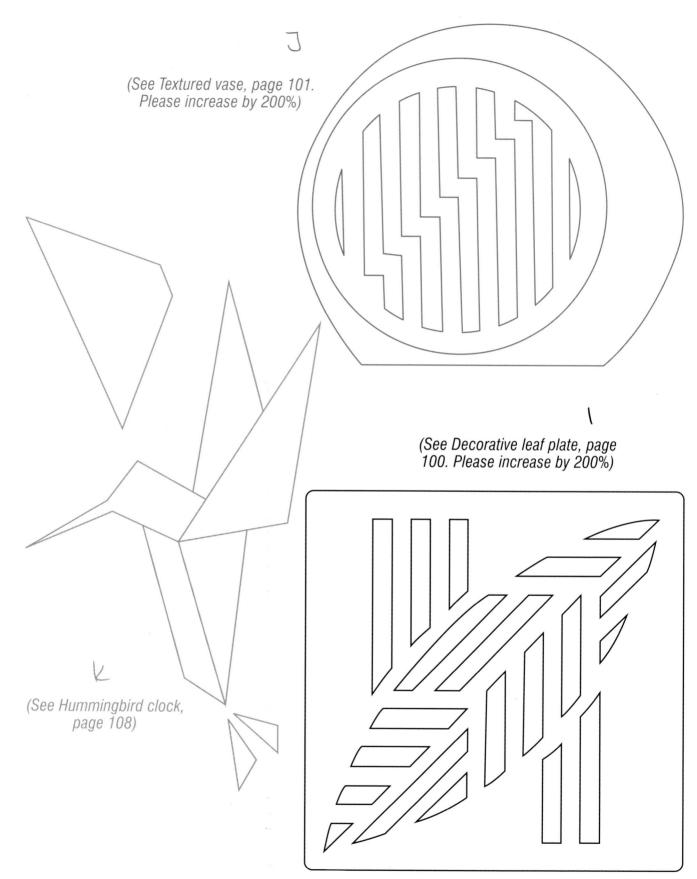

J

*(See Textured vase, page 101.
Please increase by 200%)*

\

*(See Decorative leaf plate, page
100. Please increase by 200%)*

K

*(See Hummingbird clock,
page 108)*

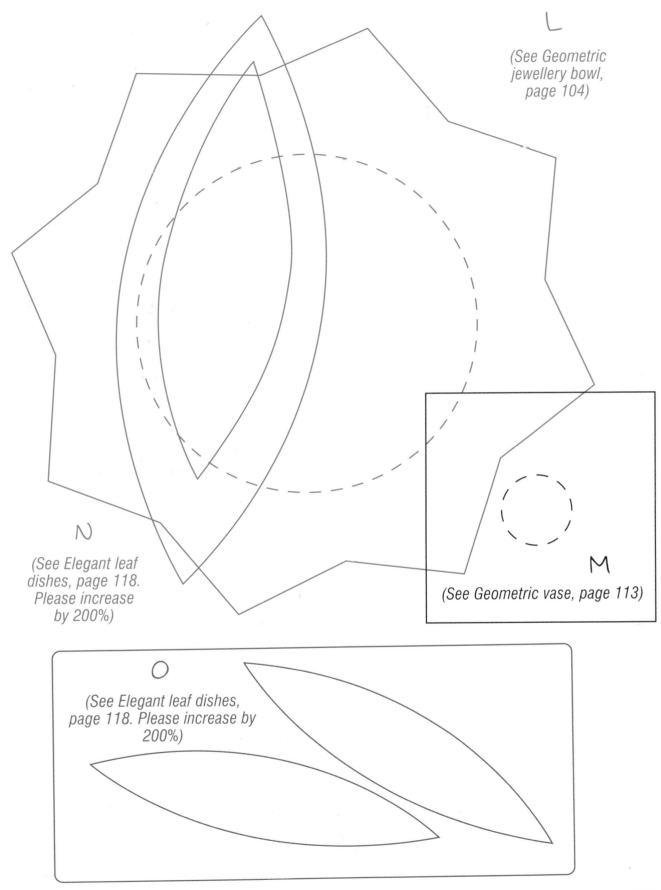

L

*(See Geometric
jewellery bowl,
page 104)*

N

*(See Elegant leaf
dishes, page 118.
Please increase
by 200%)*

M

(See Geometric vase, page 113)

O

*(See Elegant leaf dishes,
page 118. Please increase by
200%)*

The contributors

Marion Dawidowski

Marion Dawidowski is an all-rounder who loves to find ways to create and realise her myriad ideas and designs with any material she can get her hands on. She makes a living through her passion by writing many helpful handbooks on craft, and has written over more than 80 titles on a wide variety of subjects from sewing to interior design.

Marion is married, has two adult sons and a dog. She lives in Brockhagen near Bielefeld, Germany, and will happily tell you about the exciting history behind her home.

Annette Diepolder

Annette Diepolder is a designer who specialises in creating unique, handmade decorations, jewellery and accessories, and enjoys using the most diverse materials and techniques she can find – she is always keen to experiment with something new! Besides working hard in her own studio, Annette also regularly contributes to craft magazines and holds highly sought-after workshops on recent trends and styles in design.

Annette lives in Villingen-Schwenningen, in the south west of Germany.

Simea Gut

Simea Gut has always liked to be creative: painting, decorating, furnishing ... DIY is her world. She lives with her family in Lörrach, Germany on the border of Switzerland, and has a studio where she offers creative courses. She shares her passion for creativity in her blog (www.artisserie.net), and is a successful book and magazine author.

Ingrid Moras

Creative author Ingrid Moras is skilled in many crafts, including silk and fabric painting; paper, wood, wire and mosaic work; jewellery making and – of course – creating designs with the new trend material, concrete.

Ingrid is married with two adult daughters. She finds relaxation and inspiration in her garden, and enjoys hiking in her homeland, the Allgäu, in southern Germany.

Elke Reith

Elke Reith is a professional textile designer and photo stylist. She has contributed to many craft magazines, and written several books on a wide variety of subjects including sewing, knitting, crochet and felt.

Sybille Rogaczewski-Nogai

Sybille Rogaczewski-Nogai is a primary school teacher who specialises in fine art and textile work. She has published several successful titles in Germany, with a number geared towards encouraging children to explore the world of art and craft.